YOU CHOOSE BOOKS™

MEXICAN IMMIGRANTS IN AMERICA

An Interactive History Adventure

by Rachael Hanel

Consultant:
Anne M. Martínez
Assistant Professor of History
University of Texas at Austin

Capstone
press®

Mankato, Minnesota

You Choose Books are published by Capstone Press,
151 Good Counsel Drive, P.O. Box 669, Mankato, Minnesota 56002.
www.capstonepress.com

Library of Congress Cataloging-in-Publication Data
Hanel, Rachael.
    Mexican immigrants in America : an interactive history adventure / by Rachael Hanel.
    p. cm. — (You choose books)
    Includes bibliographical references and index.
    Summary: "Describes the experiences of Mexican citizens who immigrate to America legally
and illegally. The reader's choices reveal historical and modern details about where they settled, the
jobs they found, and the difficulties they faced" — Provided by publisher.
        ISBN-13: 978-1-4296-2013-0 (hardcover)   ISBN-13: 978-1-4296-2865-5 (softcover)
        ISBN-10: 1-4296-2013-7 (hardcover)   ISBN-10: 1-4296-2865-0 (softcover)
        1. Mexican Americans — History — Juvenile literature. 2. Mexicans — United States —
History — Juvenile literature. 3. Immigrants — United States — History — Juvenile literature.
4. Mexican Americans — Social conditions — Juvenile literature. 5. Mexicans — United States
— Social conditions — Juvenile literature. 6. Immigrants — United States — Social conditions
— Juvenile literature. 7. Mexico — Emigration and immigration — Juvenile literature. 8. United
States — Emigration and immigration — Juvenile literature. I. Title. II. Series.
E184.M5H363 2009
973.046872 — dc22   2008004359

Editorial Credits
Jennifer Besel, editor; Juliette Peters, set designer; Patrick Dentinger, book designer; Danielle
    Ceminsky, illustrator; Wanda Winch, photo researcher

Photo Credits
Alamy/AlanHaynes.com, 74; Alamy/Jeff Greenberg, 95; Alamy/Jim West, cover; Alamy/Keith
Dannemiller, 70; AP Images/Damian Dovarganes, 83, 103; AP Images/Jose Luis Magana, 76;
AP Images/Matt York, 53, 100, 105; AP Images/Pecos Enterprise, Jon Fulbright, 60; Corbis/
Annie Griffiths Belt, 42; Corbis/Danny Lehman, 12, 18; Corbis/Ed Kashi, 56; Corbis/Morton
Beebe, 17; Getty Images Inc./Bob Parent, 39; Getty Images Inc./David McNew, 81; Getty
Images Inc./Tim Boyle, 67; Landov LLC/MCT/Tom Pennington, 45; Landov LLC/UPI/Earl
S. Cryer, 99; Magnum Photos/Paul Fusco, 34; Peter Arnold Inc./Mark Edwards, 6; Richard
M. Hackett, 91; Shutterstock/Mark Scott Spatny, 63; Shutterstock/Pierdelune, 49; Walter P.
Reuther Library/Wayne State University, 24, 27, 30, 37; Walter P. Reuther Library/Wayne
State University/Cathy Murphy Photo, 21

TABLE OF CONTENTS

About Your
Adventure

YOU are a young Mexican citizen, struggling to put food on the table. But just to the north lies one of the world's wealthiest nations. You cross the U.S. border, hoping to bring a better life to you and your family. Will you succeed?

In this book, you'll explore how the choices people made meant the difference between life and death. The events you'll experience happened to real people.

Chapter One sets the scene. Then you choose which path to read. Follow the directions at the bottom of each page. The choices you make will change your outcome. After you finish one path, go back and read the others for new perspectives.

YOU CHOOSE the path
you take through history.

People in Mexican villages struggle to find work that will pay them enough money to survive.

LEAVING HOME

You stand outside your tiny house and look around. The mountains here in Mexico are beautiful. But life is hard and you're frustrated. The economy is poor. It's nearly impossible to earn enough money to feed your family. Small villages like yours consist of homes that are not much more than shacks. Some don't even have running water. Children are forced to leave school in order to work.

Turn the page.

Just across Mexico's northern border lies one of the wealthiest countries in the world — the United States. Everyone here calls it *el Norte*, Spanish for the North. You think often of going there. You know several people who have gone to the United States to work. They send money back to their families. Most of them dream of returning to Mexico one day to live off the money they've earned. The U.S. dollar goes a long way in Mexico. Even a low-paying job in the States would earn you more than a job here.

Yet you know getting into the United States is risky. The U.S. government doesn't hand out many residency visas to people from Mexico. That's the only way to get into the country legally. You've checked at the consulate. The consul told you the wait for a visa is seven to 10 years.

Many people you know have entered the United States illegally. You have a friend who tried crossing the border. But he was caught and returned to the village.

"I'm going to keep trying," he tells you. "I want to work in the United States. There's nothing for me here."

Turn the page.

You've heard stories of how tough life can be up there. Immigration is a hot topic among Americans. Some Americans think there should be extra border patrols to keep Mexican immigrants out. You've also heard stories of racism. Is the move worth it?

Eventually, you decide that it is. Your family needs your help. They are hungry. There is no future for them. You decide to take the risk and go north. The United States holds the promise of a better life for you and your family.

The immigrant experience is different for every person. Everyone faces many decisions. Your first decision will be where to go.

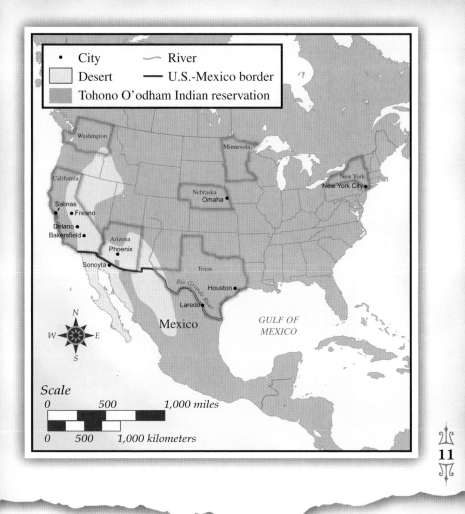

➤ To experience life as a migrant worker in the 1970s,
turn to page **13**.

➤ To become a domestic worker in the early 21st century,
turn to page **43**.

➤ To work in a modern-day meatpacking plant,
turn to page **71**.

Many Mexican citizens live in shacks because they cannot afford better housing.

CHAPTER 2

LIFE IN THE FIELDS

For several weeks, you've been saving your money. You're going to get to the United States one way or another.

"There's no future for us here," you tell your wife. "I hear farm work is available for us in the United States. I think it's time to move." You both will be sad to leave your parents, brothers, and sisters. But your two small children are often hungry. You want to provide for your family.

One day, a recruiter for U.S. growers comes through town. He promises jobs in the States.

Turn the page.

"Growers in the United States need many workers," the recruiter says. "Crops like grapes and peas are growing there like never before. There's so much work that the U.S. government will give you a visa right away."

You listen more closely. You know that getting a visa to enter the country legally is usually very difficult.

"You'll make good money. There's never been a better time to move to the States."

Later you and a few others gather at your neighbor's house.

"I like this idea," you say. "We can get in legally. Without this permit, we will have to wait many more years to get a visa."

Your neighbor shakes his head. "I don't know. My brother worked for a recruiter. He was promised a lot of money, but the recruiter didn't pay him as much as promised. The recruiters tell you where to work and where to live. I think I would rather go across the border myself and find work on my own. You should come with me. My brother told me the way to go."

You think about what your neighbor said. What if he's right about the recruiter? But if you try to cross illegally, you might be caught.

➼ *To take a job with the recruiter, turn to page* **16**.
➼ *To cross with your neighbor, turn to page* **18**.

The next morning, you find the recruiter and sign up. After a few days, the list is full. You and your family board buses to the United States.

The buses cross the border in a caravan. The ride is very hot. The grower is expecting all of you right away. You only stop once every few hours.

After more than 40 hours on the bus, you arrive in Fresno, California. This is the heart of produce country. You see nothing but fields.

"How does anything grow in the desert?" your wife asks.

"See those metal pipes? They shoot out water. They irrigate the land," you tell her.

The recruiter talks to everyone when you arrive.

Workers stoop down all day while picking broccoli.

"Like I said, there's plenty of work available. The pea harvest is just getting started down in Bakersfield. Or you can harvest broccoli here in Fresno. Broccoli pays by the box. You get 30 cents per box. Harvesting peas pays $1.25 per hour."

You try to do the math in your head. What will pay more?

➤ To harvest peas in Bakersfield, turn to page **20**.

➤ To harvest broccoli in Fresno, turn to page **23**.

Hundreds of people wait until night to try to cross the U.S. border.

You decide to cross with your neighbor. You and your neighbor load your families on a bus. You travel to the desert of northwestern Mexico, just across the border from California. You wait until nightfall to cross. For hours, you hike across the soft desert sand. Your back is sore from carrying your youngest child.

When the sun rises, you come to a town. You've made it to the United States. Now you must get to Delano. There your neighbor's brother works in the grape fields. At a small diner, you see a pickup truck with Mexicans in the back.

"We'd like to go to Delano," you say. "Are you going that way?"

"Actually," says one of the men, "we're going to Salinas to harvest lettuce. There's threat of a strike in the grape fields. We're not sure if there's work there. There's a better chance to work if you harvest lettuce."

Do you stay with your neighbor and go to Delano? Or should you try harvesting lettuce?

➤ To go to Salinas to harvest lettuce, turn to page **26**.

➤ To go to Delano with your neighbor, turn to page **29**.

You decide to try picking peas. Another bus takes you south to Bakersfield. The crew leader puts both you and your wife to work. Your 7-year-old son and 5-year-old daughter work too.

You walk in a bent position, picking peas and tossing them into a basket. After a few hours, every muscle aches. It hurts to stand, and it hurts to stoop. But you work through the pain.

You take your full basket to the crew leader.

"We only want good peas," he says. He removes a third of the peas and throws them on the ground. You didn't think there was anything wrong with those peas. But you take the basket back into the field and pick until it's full.

Even young children worked long hours in the fields to make money for their families.

At dusk, you hobble to a makeshift camp located just outside the fields. All the workers live here in one-room plywood shacks. The shacks are empty except for a little stove and mattresses on the floor. Dozens of workers share one outdoor toilet.

The next day, your wife and children are coughing. It's probably because of the pesticides, chemicals owners spray on the fields to keep insects away.

Turn the page.

In addition to a cough, one of your coworkers has terrible back pain. He can't stand up straight.

"We can't work in these conditions," you say to him. "We should complain to the crew leader."

"No, please don't say anything!" the man begs. "If he knows I'm hurt, he won't let me work. Then I won't make any money. Please stay quiet. I will work through it."

You think your boss should know about this. But maybe your coworker is right. Maybe it's best to stay quiet. You've seen extra workers line up at the gates each day. You could be replaced at any moment.

➤ *To stay quiet, turn to page* **32**.

➤ *To complain to your crew leader, turn to page* **35**.

At the broccoli farm, you see many other migrants waiting for work. You find the crew leader.

"You said there would be plenty of work," you tell him. "It looks like there are too many people here."

"I don't know when other groups will show up," he replies. "That's the life of a migrant."

But you and your wife are strong. You have children who can also work. The crew leader picks your family to work in these fields.

You bend low as you walk through the broccoli rows. Using a small knife, you cut the large center stem of each plant. You work quickly, trying to harvest the broccoli before the yellow flowers blossom.

Turn the page.

At night, you shuffle to the makeshift camp set up by the workers. Each house is just a one-room shack with a dirt floor. Everyone shares an outdoor toilet.

After a few days, you have a nagging cough. Your wife and children are coughing too. Other workers have skin rashes.

"What is happening?" you ask another worker.

Most farmworkers could not afford to live anywhere but the poor camps near the fields.

"It's the pesticides," he says. "The grower sprays the fields with chemicals to keep insects away. We breathe in the chemicals, and they get on our skin."

"This isn't right," you say. "My children are very sick. We shouldn't have to work in these conditions."

"What are you going to do about it?" your coworker asks. "If you complain, you might be fired. The grower will never change anything, anyway. You might as well just work and earn your wage."

What should you do? Should you complain to the crew leader and risk your job? Or should you just keep working and stay quiet?

➤ To stay quiet and continue working, turn to page 32.

➤ To complain about the working conditions, turn to page 35.

The man was right. There's plenty of work in the lettuce fields. But it's hard work. You stoop low to the ground, cutting the lettuce out of the soil with a sharp knife. Your back aches and you're so thirsty. The grower doesn't provide much drinking water.

At night, you go to your temporary home, one of the many shacks at the edge of the field. Your shack has just one room and a dirt floor. Everyone shares one outside toilet.

You hear others talk about joining a union.

"Cesar Chavez is a smart man," says a coworker. "He will fight for our rights. We deserve better wages and better housing."

"Already Chavez's United Farm Workers union has won some fights with growers," another worker says.

Cesar Chavez (front center) and the UFW signed contracts with growers that improved wages and working conditions.

"But if we join the UFW," someone argues, "we might be fired. You know the growers get to choose our union. And they're talking with the Teamsters. The Teamsters will help the growers keep wages low."

The next day, representatives from the Teamsters union talk to you and your coworkers.

Turn the page.

"The growers have signed a Teamsters contract," one of the organizers says. "If you don't join our union, you will be fired."

If you want to keep your job, you have to follow the grower's choice and become a Teamster. But others are planning to fight the growers and join the UFW. Chavez and other leaders are promising to get you better wages. Do you take the risk?

➤ *To join the Teamsters, turn to page 38.*

➤ *To join the UFW, turn to page 39.*

You decide to go to Delano to find work with your neighbor. Some grape fields are not affected by strikes, so you manage to get a job.

You and your family work long and hard in the grape fields. You grab a large metal tub and knife and begin work. Crawling on your knees, you use both hands to cut the bunches of green globes off the vines. You work for hours. When your tub is finally full, you empty it into a large vat and begin again.

Soon after you arrive, the grower signs a contract with Cesar Chavez's United Farm Workers union (UFW). Your pay increases to $1.80 per hour. That's double what you were making.

Turn the page.

Unfortunately, the good times don't last. The contract expires in 1973. Most of the growers, including the one you work for, sign contracts with the Teamsters union. The Teamsters work with the growers, keeping wages very low.

Chavez calls on all workers to go on strike. You decide to strike with the others. One day, Chavez arrives to speak to all of you. In your mind, he is larger than life. But you're surprised he is so small. His face looks worn and tired.

Cesar Chavez (front center) stood on the picket lines with workers, peacefully demonstrating for workers' rights.

"Thank you for being a part of the strike," Chavez says to you. "We couldn't fight without you. But we really need some people to stand on the picket lines. It's important to show the growers and the citizens of the United States that we're serious."

You pause. "I'm not sure. I've heard there's been violence against protesters."

Chavez nods. "That's true. There are dangers. But that makes picketing even more important. It shows that we're determined to win this fight with nonviolence."

You think about what Chavez said. Do you demonstrate, or do you quietly go on strike?

→ *To demonstrate on the picket line, turn to page **34**.*

→ *To strike quietly, turn to page **36**.*

You decide not to say anything. You've seen the crew leader fire those who complain. You know you should be grateful to have a job.

Month after month, year after year, you follow the crew leader to different fields. In the summer, you go north to Washington to harvest apples. In the winter, you come back to southern California. The housing everywhere is terrible. Every year, your cough worsens.

After 15 years, you feel like an old man. Breathing is difficult. Your lungs feel like they are coated in cement. You finally go to a doctor at a free clinic.

"The pesticides are killing you," she says. "You have lung cancer. You have only a few months to live."

You think of your children. You brought them to the United States so they could have a better life. But they have to work in the fields as hard as you do. You think they will never have the chance to go to college.

Your doctor gives you some frightening information. The average lifespan of a migrant worker is just 49 years. Most Americans live to be 74 years old. Each year, an estimated 1,000 workers die from pesticide poisoning. You soon will be one of those statistics.

THE END

To follow another path, turn to page 11.
To read the conclusion, turn to page 101.

Union members held signs that said *huelga*. *Huelga* means strike in Spanish.

You join hundreds of others on the picket line. You shout *"Viva la causa!* Long live the cause!" The police harass you. Other people throw rocks. Chavez tells you to stay strong.

You find out a judge has ruled the picketing illegal. Soon police arrest you. You remember back to 1970 when Chavez was jailed for not stopping a lettuce boycott. If he can go to jail for *la Causa,* so can you. You vow to always fight for workers' rights.

THE END

To follow another path, turn to page 11.
To read the conclusion, turn to page 101.

The conditions are too bad to ignore.

"I am upset about these working conditions," you tell your crew leader. "We deserve better."

The crew leader shakes his head. "If you don't like it, you're fired."

You and your family leave the farm. At the next town, you meet some other Mexican immigrants.

"You can join us," one says. "We're going north to work in the fruit harvest."

You join them. Month after month, you move to follow the harvests — apples, broccoli, grapes, and peas. You try to save money from each job. You hope some day to buy a house and have a real home to go back to.

THE END

To follow another path, turn to page 11.
To read the conclusion, turn to page 101.

You don't want to take a chance on the picket lines. You and your family strike quietly. You survive on the $5 a week the union pays strikers. It's barely enough for food and a few clothes.

By the summer of 1973, violence toward picketers is out of control. You fear for your coworkers. In August, you get word that two strikers have been killed. You don't know Nagi Daifullah. But as you hear the second name, tears well up in your eyes. Juan de la Cruz had been a good friend to you. You had worked side by side in the grape fields. Now he had died fighting for workers' rights.

It takes a long time, but eventually the strike is resolved. Chavez has an friend in California Governor Jerry Brown. In 1975, Brown signs the Agricultural Labor Relations Act (ALRA).

Jerry Brown (at microphone) worked with Chavez and other leaders to improve working conditions.

This law lets workers choose their union. The ALRA also sets up a board to help solve problems between growers and workers.

Slowly the workers make progress. You go back to work with higher wages and safer working conditions. The union's work has helped make your job safer.

THE END

To follow another path, turn to page 11.
To read the conclusion, turn to page 101.

37

You join the Teamsters. You can't afford to be out of work. But many of your coworkers join Chavez's UFW.

"Traitor!" one of your coworkers says to you. "As long as the grower can hire Teamsters labor, the workers will never get ahead!"

You feel guilty. You want better wages, but you also need money right now.

Teamsters officials constantly battle with UFW representatives. Chavez calls for citizens to boycott lettuce. Lettuce sales drop, and you find yourself out of a job anyway. If you had known you would lose your job, you would have joined the UFW in the first place.

You join the UFW and fight for your rights as a farmworker. With 7,000 other lettuce workers, you go on strike. You yell, "*Viva la causa!* Long live the cause!" At the same time, the UFW continues to tell people not to buy nonunion lettuce. The growers are not pleased with this. The boycott causes them to lose a lot of money.

Nationwide boycotts were an effective nonviolent way to get growers' attention.

Turn the page.

In December 1970, some growers convince a judge to have Chavez arrested for not stopping the boycott. He is locked in jail for 14 days.

As the lettuce harvest comes to a close, so does your strike. You go back to work, harvesting broccoli, tomatoes, onions, and peppers. The work is hard and hurts your body. It seems with all the fighting, not much has changed. You realize working conditions will not improve overnight. This will be a long fight.

But by the mid-1970s, California has a new governor, Jerry Brown. Brown is sympathetic to Chavez and the United Farm Workers. In 1975, California passes a law called the Agricultural Labor Relations Act (ALRA).

The ALRA allows unions to strike at harvest time. A committee is set up to hear disputes between growers and workers. Best of all, it allows workers to vote for their unions. Growers can't choose the unions anymore. Not surprisingly, Chavez's union wins most of the elections.

Working conditions slowly improve. The ALRA was a big step. You have already seen higher wages and better housing. You're confident that Chavez and the other UFW leaders will always fight for your rights.

THE END

To follow another path, turn to page 11.
To read the conclusion, turn to page 101.

People in poor Mexican villages wash their clothes in rivers full of chemicals dumped from factories.

CHAPTER 3

WORKING FOR SEÑORA

"Shhhh, shhhh, it's going to be OK." You stroke your daughter's tear-streaked cheek.

"But mama, I'm hungry!" she wails.

For the third night in a row, supper was just a glass of water with a teaspoon of sugar. You hoped the sugar would be enough to quiet your children's stomachs. It isn't.

It's been several weeks since your husband died. You alone must support your children in this southern Mexican village. But the only job you can find is washing other people's clothes at the river. This job pays very little.

43

Turn the page.

You know there's work in *los Estados*, the States. But the only way to get to the States right away is to enter illegally. There's no way you can wait seven to 10 years for a visa. Your children are starving now. You will do what thousands of others do each year. You'll borrow what little money your mother and siblings have. Then you'll pay a man called a coyote to smuggle you across the border.

But before you go, you have to make one important decision. Will you take your son and daughter with you now, or will you send for them in a few months? The crossing is dangerous. It might be easier to go to the United States first and establish a home there. But can you leave your children behind?

➤ *To cross with your children, go to page* **45**.

➤ *To cross alone and leave your children behind, turn to page* **48**.

44

The crossing might be risky, but you'd rather stay together. You take a bus to a town just across the border from Laredo, Texas. There you'll cross the Rio Grande River.

The coyote knows a narrow, shallow area of the river where you can cross. You carry your daughter on your back. The coyote carries your son. Luckily, the entire group makes it safely across. You're now in the United States.

Many people risk their lives crossing the Rio Grande River in an attempt to enter the United States.

Turn the page.

One of the first things you do is find an employment agency in Laredo. This agency helps immigrants find work. You get a job as a housekeeper in Houston. With the little money you have left, you take a bus to Houston and find a small apartment.

Your job is cleaning a huge home for a wealthy señora. You work long hours mopping and dusting. Your children are small, so you have to take them with you while you work. Your new employer doesn't like that.

"The agency didn't say you'd be bringing your children," she snaps. "Don't let them get into anything."

You can't understand a word of English, and the señora doesn't speak Spanish. But she screams a lot.

One day you take an apple off the counter to feed your children.

"Did you take an apple?" the señora questions. Through hand gestures, you figure out what she's saying. "That's stealing! I don't pay you to steal food from me!"

You don't like her, but this is your only way to earn money. Besides, you are starting to learn some English. With more English skills, maybe you'll be able to find a better job later.

One morning, your daughter wakes up very sick. She coughs and can hardly breathe. You need to stay home with her. But will the señora fire you for taking time off?

→ *To ask for time off, turn to page* **50**.

→ *To go to work, turn to page* **52**.

Leaving your children behind is the hardest thing you've ever done. But during your journey to the States, you realize how hard it would have been to cross with them. The crossing is rough. You and a dozen others follow a coyote across the Rio Grande River into Texas. As you cross, the woman next to you is swept away in the current. No one is able to save her. The same thing could have happened to your son or daughter.

You become friends with Rosa, another woman on the journey.

"I'm going to New York City," she says. "My cousin works as a housekeeper there. She says there are many rich people. Do you want to come with me?"

You don't know anyone else, so you go to the biggest city in the United States.

Immigrants find many opportunities in New York City.

New York City is more than you ever imagined. Lights in the huge skyscrapers twinkle against the night sky. Taxis honk their horns. People crowd the streets. This huge city is exciting, but it's a bit scary too. You've never seen anything like it.

Turn to page 54.

You call your employer. "Señora, my daughter is very sick. May I stay home today?"

"Sure, you can stay home," she says. "But if you do, don't bother coming back."

You don't have a choice. You must stay home with your sick daughter. The next day, you visit an employment agency to find a new job. While you wait, you talk with another immigrant named Elsy.

"I'm meeting with a lawyer today to try to get permanent residency," she says. "The lawyer told me that I should get other immigrants together. With more people, she can give us a deal on her services. Are you interested?"

You can't really afford a lawyer right now. But on the other hand, you want to work toward legal status. You don't want to be a housekeeper the rest of your life, hiding from the law.

→ To turn down Elsy's offer, turn to page **62**.

→ To hire the lawyer, turn to page **64**.

You can't risk losing your job, so you go to work. You set your daughter on a cot in the pantry and check on her often. Your son helps you with little jobs around the house.

When the señora comes into the kitchen, your daughter coughs. Your employer glares at you. She marches to the pantry.

"You brought your sick daughter here?" she screams. "Get out! You're fired!"

A few nights later, there's a knock at your apartment door. You open the door to find two men standing there.

"Ma'am, we are from Immigration and Customs Enforcement. We received word you might be here illegally. Can we see your papers?"

You don't have papers. The agents take you and your children to a detention center. There you're put on a bus and taken back to Mexico.

You make your way back to your village. You know you can't stay, though. You start planning how to get back to the United States.

Hundreds of illegal Mexican immigrants are brought back to Mexico each day.

THE END

To follow another path, turn to page 11.
To read the conclusion, turn to page 101.

You find an employment agency that works with immigrants. You go to several interviews. No one asks if you're legal or not. After a few days, a couple hires you as a nanny in their large apartment overlooking Central Park.

"We can let you stay in a spare room," the woman says. "We will pay you $150 per week."

Your eyes light up. That money will go a long way in Mexico when you send it to your mother, who's watching your children.

After a few weeks in the city, you find the courage to go out and explore. You meet other immigrants and soon become part of the immigrant community.

You want to do something in your spare time to help your children. Maybe you could get a second job. You could make more money and bring your kids here sooner. Or maybe you should take English classes. Learning the language will help you understand this country better.

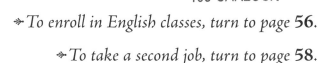

↠ *To enroll in English classes, turn to page **56**.*

↠ *To take a second job, turn to page **58**.*

You look around the room at everyone else who signed up for English class. There are so many people. They speak many different languages.

"Are you nervous?" a woman next to you asks in Spanish.

You're relieved someone else here speaks Spanish. "I'm afraid I won't be able to learn English. It sounds so hard."

For many immigrants, learning English helps them get better jobs in United States.

The woman nods. "But think of how much easier it will be once we know the language."

After a few months, you know enough English to read the newspaper and speak to the cashiers at the grocery store. You think about starting your own housecleaning business. Your employer lines up some clients for you. Before long, you're turning down cleaning jobs because you have too many.

Turn to page 59.

You believe taking a second job is the best way to get your children here as quickly as possible. You go into a Mexican restaurant one night.

"Excuse me," you say to the cashier. "Do you have any jobs available?"

"As a matter of fact, we do," she says. "One of our waitresses just quit. How soon can you start?"

You start the next night. Your days and weeks blend together because you're so busy. You work as a nanny until 6:00 in the evening, then you waitress at night. Many nights you get only four or five hours of sleep. But you remember your children and know the sacrifice is worth it.

You've finally saved enough money to bring your children here. You can get them here one of two ways. You can go back to Mexico and bring them here yourself. Or you can pay to have a coyote smuggle them across the border.

Both decisions could be dangerous. If you return to Mexico, you might not make it back. And leaving means giving up the jobs you've worked so hard for. But if you pay someone to smuggle your children into the States, they will be taking a dangerous journey without you. You've heard horror stories where children are robbed and beaten. Can you trust the coyote?

❧ To go to Mexico to get your children, turn to page **60**.

❧ To hire a coyote, turn to page **68**.

"I can't let someone else bring my children here," you tell your friend Rosa.

Rosa nods. "I understand. Did you hear about the immigrants who died because they were crammed into the back of a truck? It got so hot that they suffocated."

It takes you several days to get back to your village. Your children run to greet you.

Immigrants hide in the back of trucks crossing the border. U.S. Border Patrol agents search vehicles for hidden people.

"Please don't leave us again, Mama," says your son.

"I won't," you say.

You find a coyote in your village. "How much to take me and my two children?" you ask him.

"It will be $3,000."

"What?" you say with surprise. "But I saved only $2,000!"

You leave his house in tears. What will you do now? You could go back to the States and try to earn more money. But you promised your children you wouldn't leave them. You find yourself back where you started.

THE END

To follow another path, turn to page 11.
To read the conclusion, turn to page 101.

"I don't have enough money right now," you tell Elsy. "I don't want to take out a loan. I'll look into getting residency in a few months."

The agency sets you up with a new job. This time, you're going to be a nanny. You and your children will live in your employer's big house.

This señora is much nicer than the last one. She lets you eat food from her kitchen. She also pays well. You earn $200 each week.

At the park, you meet other domestic workers who work nearby. While the children play, one worker, Delores, tells you about an upcoming event.

"On May 1, people are going to protest tougher laws against immigrants," she says. "The protests are going to happen all around the country. There are millions of immigrants. What if we all took the day off from work? Then Americans will see how much we mean to the economy."

You and Delores go downtown on May 1. Thousands of immigrants and U.S. citizens stand together, working for a common goal.

Immigrants and citizens gather together each year on May 1 to work toward more rights for immigrants.

↠ *Turn to page 67.*

You decide not to wait. You and Elsy meet with the lawyer.

"I can file the paperwork to make you legal in one month," she says. "It's going to cost you $5,000."

You gasp. How will you raise that much money? The lawyer says you can get a loan from a bank. "I need $3,000 right away," she says. "You can pay the rest later when you are legal."

Even though you are illegal, it's easy to find a bank to loan you the money. There are millions of illegal immigrants in the United States, and banks are eager to attract business. You pay the lawyer, and she gives you official-looking papers to sign. But after a month, you still don't have residency.

"There's been a delay," the lawyer says. "I need the rest of the money."

You take out another loan for the rest of the money. Another week passes. Then two. You hear nothing from the lawyer. Neither does Elsy. You both decide to visit her.

Turn the page.

You get to the lawyer's office. The door is locked. You peer through the window. All the desks and file cabinets are gone.

"I doubt she was even a lawyer," cries Elsy. "She took all our money!"

You are scared. Now you owe $5,000 to the bank. How could you have been so trusting? If you don't pay the bank, they'll report you to Immigration and Customs Enforcement. You figure you might as well go back to Mexico. At least there no one will be looking for you. You'll have to find another way to feed your family.

THE END

To follow another path, turn to page 11.
To read the conclusion, turn to page 101.

You return from the rally full of energy. In your spare time, you volunteer at a center that helps illegal immigrants get medical care and legal advice. After weeks of volunteering, you're offered a full-time job. With the money you earn, you hire a lawyer whom you trust. You know that one day, you and your children will be U.S. citizens. The long wait will be worth it.

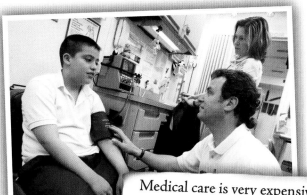

Medical care is very expensive. Centers that offer free care are often the only option for immigrants.

THE END

To follow another path, turn to page 11.
To read the conclusion, turn to page 101.

"Paying a coyote to bring your children here is scary," says your friend Rosa.

"Yes, I'm terribly frightened," you admit. "But if I leave, I will lose my jobs and will have to start from scratch."

You wire money to your mother. She pays a coyote to bring your children across the border.

You take a bus to Texas to meet them at the border town of Laredo. You check into a motel when you arrive. But you can't sleep. What if something happens to them? You think back to the woman who died crossing the river.

The next morning, you go to the bus station. You had your mother tell the coyote that you would meet them here. You wait all day, but there's no sign of them. You watch the clock tick away the hours. The next morning finally arrives. Where are they?

You put your head in your hands and sob. If your children have died or are missing, how will you ever know?

Just then, there's a tap on your shoulder. You look up through tear-filled eyes. There before you are your two children!

"Oh, my babies!" you cry, wrapping them in big hugs. You laugh and cry out of joy.

"We're finally together," you say, kissing them. "Wait until you see what New York is like! We will make a new life there, just the three of us."

THE END

To follow another path, turn to page 11.
To read the conclusion, turn to page 101.

Many young men leave their villages to find work in Mexico City.

CHAPTER 4

CROSSING TO OMAHA

You're 20 years old. You live in a small village but work a few hours away in Mexico City. You make $130 per week. It's not enough to support your large family. Your mother is sick and cannot work. Your father died years ago. Your younger siblings are forced to drop out of school to take low-paying jobs.

"Mama, I'm going to the United States," you tell your mother. "I will send money home to you."

Your mother cries, but nods her head. "I will miss you," she says. "But you're our only hope for a better life."

Turn the page.

You can go to the United States one of two ways. You heard on the radio that a big meatpacking plant in Omaha, Nebraska, is hiring workers from Mexico. The company will give you a temporary visa to work for six months. After that, you will have to go home. But can you earn enough money in six months?

Or you can hire a man, called a coyote, to take you into the United States illegally. You can stay as long as you want, as long as you're not caught. Your cousin already lives in Omaha. He says he can get you a job at a meatpacking plant. What will you do?

➤ *To enter legally, go to page* **73**.

➤ *To enter illegally, turn to page* **75**.

The radio ad said there's a recruiter's office in Sonoyta, a town in northern Mexico. You take a bus ride to the office. All you carry is a small suitcase with a few changes of clothes. You find the office and walk in.

"I heard you were looking for workers," you tell the man at the desk. "I would like to sign up."

You sign some papers and wait in the small room for hours. More men come in to sign up. Soon the waiting room is full.

"OK, we're ready to go," a man tells you. "The van is waiting outside."

The trip to Omaha takes two days. You can go to the bathroom and get food only when the van stops for gas.

Turn the page.

Many workers live in poor housing so they can send more money to their families in Mexico.

In Omaha, the van stops in front of a run-down house.

"Here's your new home," the driver says.

Inside it looks as if the carpet hasn't been vacuumed for years. Mattresses are thrown on the floor. Paint flakes off the walls. You'll all be living here.

The next morning, you report for work.

Turn to page 78.

You know a coyote in Mexico City who can help you cross. "How much to get across the border?" you ask.

"It will cost you $2,000," Ricardo, the coyote, says. Your eyes widen. That's everything you've saved over the past few months.

In Mexico City, you board a bus with several others. This bus will take you to the town of Sonoyta on the Mexico-Arizona border. After the 34-hour trip, you spend the night at a motel.

The next morning, a taxi drops you off in the desert. You hope *la migra*, the U.S. Border Patrol, doesn't see you cross. Each person in your group carries two bottles of water. All of you share just six limes and a few cans of beans and sardines.

Turn the page.

You walk through the sandy desert for hours. The sun beats down. You feel like you're going to faint. Your throat screams for water, but you take sips to conserve what little you have. Then you hear screaming behind you.

"Maria has fallen!" someone shouts.

You run back to see what is going on. You sat next to Maria on the bus, but now she is barely breathing.

Immigrants walk for hours in the hot, dry desert. Often they have no map, just their coyote to lead the way.

"She needs help," you say. "Otherwise she might die. Someone should go to the main road and get help from the Border Patrol." Everyone is quiet. They know what that means. If the Border Patrol finds you, you will have to go back to Mexico.

You know you should help the woman. But you think back to your family. They need your help too. They are depending on you to earn money. Maria is just a stranger.

→ To leave Maria and keep going, turn to page **80**.

→ To get help for Maria, turn to page **93**.

The factory is huge. Some people speak English rapidly. You have no idea what they're saying. You stick close to the people you know.

Your supervisor speaks both English and Spanish. He points you to an assembly line. You have to cut the meat off pigs.

Day after day, all you do is cut. You make the same motion with your right hand several times a minute. Your supervisor walks by often to make sure you're keeping up.

Your shoulders and back throb with pain. But there's no time to rest. You've already seen the supervisor fire a coworker. You don't want that to happen to you. You make $8 per hour, and $16 per hour for overtime. This is less than American workers earn. The boss knows he can hire Mexican workers for less. But to you, this is good money.

One day, Jorge, a guy who works next to you, gets hurt. His knife slips and he cuts his hand deeply. You call for the supervisor.

"I told you to be careful!" the supervisor yells at Jorge. "Go to the nurse's office here. Be back in an hour."

That cut looked serious to you. You think Jorge should see a doctor. Maybe you should report Jorge's accident to a higher manager. But then again, maybe it's best to stay silent. If you speak up, they might send you back to Mexico. What should you do?

❧ *To complain to a manager, turn to page* **84**.

❧ *To stay quiet, turn to page* **86**.

"Can't someone help her?" you ask.

"I'll stay," one of the other men says. You're grateful that someone decided to stay behind. "*Gracias*," you tell him.

You continue through the desert, following Ricardo. Ricardo leads you to the Tohono O'odham Indian reservation just across the border. The reservation is quiet. It's a good spot to arrange further transportation. A few hours later, a van shows up to take you to Phoenix, Arizona.

In Phoenix, you're on your own. You arrange transportation with one of the companies that secretly transport immigrants across the States. Before long, you're on another van trip. You're headed for Omaha.

Hundreds of immigrants cross through the Tohono O'odham Indian reservation each year. The reservation is right on the Mexico-U.S. border.

Turn the page.

When you get to Omaha, you call your cousin. He lets you live in his apartment with him and his roommate, Jorge. Your cousin has a few things to tell you.

"I suggest that we get some false papers for you," he says. "The paperwork gives you a U.S. identity and a Social Security number. It's the name and number of a person who has died. According to these papers, you'll be a legal citizen. It will be easier for you to find work. If anyone asks about you, just show them the papers."

"But I would be lying," you say.

Your cousin nods. "That's true, but this is the easiest way to live and work in the United States. A lot of people do it. It will help you avoid being caught and sent back to Mexico."

Officials say immigrants pay as little as $70 to have someone make up false paperwork.

You're not sure what to do. You would like to get a job as soon as possible. But you'd rather not lie to do it. You think of your mother and family. What's the best way to help them?

→ To refuse the false documents, turn to page **87**.

→ To get false papers, turn to page **90**.

You decide this is too important to keep quiet. The next morning, you speak to your supervisor.

"Mr. Diaz, I think Jorge should have seen a doctor yesterday. His hand still hurts very badly. I think we should have better medical care because of the dangerous work we do."

Mr. Diaz glares. "You think you should have what? Aren't you already getting enough? You have a job and a place to live. Would you make this kind of money back home?"

You shake your head.

"Well, what are you complaining about? I don't want ungrateful troublemakers working for me. Consider yourself fired."

Your mouth drops open. Now what do you do? Your temporary permit only allows you to work at this plant. Without it, you can't work legally anywhere else. But you've only been here a few weeks. That money won't last long back in Mexico.

Jorge has an idea.

"My cousin has a restaurant in Minnesota. He says I can work there. It's good money. Why don't you come with me?"

➤ *To go with Jorge, turn to page 95.*

➤ *To return to Mexico, turn to page 99.*

You decide to stay quiet. You've seen people get fired for speaking up. You stay on the job for the six months. A few nights before you're set to leave for Mexico, some of your coworkers are talking at the house.

"I'm not going back," Jorge says.

"But your permit expires soon," you say.

"I'm just going to stay. My cousin lives in Minnesota. He's opening a restaurant and he needs people to manage it. Come with me."

You would like to stay. There's a lot more opportunity here than back home. But you would be illegal. You would hate to build a life here, only to be caught and sent back.

➤ *To stay in the United States, turn to page* **95**.
➤ *To go back to Mexico, turn to page* **99**.

"I won't steal someone's identity," you tell your cousin. "I don't want false documents."

"All right, it's your choice," he says. "I'll try to get you a job at the meatpacking plant anyway."

A couple of days later, your cousin is smiling when he comes home from work.

"Good news," he tells you. "The plant really needs workers. If you go in and apply, they will probably hire you without asking if you're legal."

Turn the page.

Your cousin was right. You get a job without a problem. Your job is to clean the machinery that gets dirty from the animal parts that come down the line. You use a high-pressure hose to wash the machines. The hose is hard to control. It takes every muscle you have. Your arms feel like they're going to fall off. The chemical solution that comes out of the hose smells terrible. It makes you cough. Your nose and throat burn.

But you are earning $8 per hour. That's less than what U.S. workers get at the plant, but it's a lot more than you made in Mexico. You wire most of the money to your mother in Mexico.

You get home from work one day. Your coworker and roommate, Jorge, has an idea.

"I'm going to Minnesota. My cousin has a restaurant there. He can get me a job. He says he needs a lot of workers. I think you should leave the hard work at the plant and come with me."

You don't know anyone in Minnesota. At least here, you have your cousin. What if the restaurant doesn't do well? The meatpacking plant is steady work.

→ *To go to Minnesota, turn to page **95**.*

→ *To stay at the plant, turn to page **98**.*

"All right, I'll buy the false documents if you think it will get me work faster," you say.

In a few days, you have a Social Security card and a U.S. birth certificate. They show a name different from your own.

The documents help you get a job. Your job is to wash the machines at the meatpacking plant. It's hard work. Hot liquid chemicals come pouring out of a high-pressure hose. The chemicals burn your nose and throat. But you're making $8 an hour.

Months pass. You meet a girl, a friend of your cousin's. You date for a while and then get married. Before long, you have a baby boy. Because your son was born in the United States, he's automatically a U.S. citizen.

One day, there's a loud commotion at work. People in uniforms that say ICE are all over the plant. They yell through a megaphone, "Everyone to the cafeteria."

In the cafeteria, you're interviewed by one of the men. He works for the U.S. Immigration and Customs Enforcement.

ICE agents conduct raids on factories all across the country, looking for illegal immigrants.

Turn the page.

"Show me your papers," he says.

You show him the fake documents. He takes one look and shakes his head.

"These are fake. You're not here legally. I have to deport you to Mexico."

Your heart sinks. "But I have a baby. Is there any way I can stay?"

"You can try to fight the deportation, but you'll need to get a lawyer," he says.

What should you do? A lawyer will be expensive, but you'd like to find a way to stay with your wife and baby.

→ To hire a lawyer and fight deportation, turn to page 94.

→ To be deported and try to return to the United States later, turn to page 97.

If you don't get help for Maria, you don't know who will. "I'll find help for her," you tell the group.

You start walking back the way you came. But you quickly become lost. You have no idea where the road is. You have no water left. Night falls, and it gets cold. You're very tired, so you lie down. All you want to do is close your eyes. Without water or shelter in the desert, death comes quickly.

THE END

To follow another path, turn to page 11.
To read the conclusion, turn to page 101.

You hire a lawyer who specializes in immigration law. Her name is Christine. She's part of a network of lawyers that helps immigrants.

"I think we should say that your family would experience hardship if you were deported," Christine says. "It will be difficult for your wife to take care of your U.S. citizen son without your income. You will not be able to earn enough money in Mexico to support them."

*Turn to page **96**.*

Owning a business is a great success for some immigrants.

Going to Minnesota will be an adventure. You hope it works out. In Minnesota, Jorge's cousin hires you and Jorge to manage the restaurant. After a few months, you have enough money to bring your family to the United States. You're so happy that your family is together again.

THE END

To follow another path, turn to page 11.
To read the conclusion, turn to page 101.

It's the day of your hearing. The judge listens to Christine's argument. She presents letters from your employer, landlord, and neighbors that say you are a good person. You haven't been convicted of a crime.

The judge decides it would be a hardship for your family if you were sent back to Mexico. You get to stay. You hire Christine to help you get legal paperwork. You hope to send money to your family so they can come to the United States. You want your entire family to be together.

96

THE END

To follow another path, turn to page 11.
To read the conclusion, turn to page 101.

"I don't have any extra money," you tell the officer. "I'm not going to fight deportation."

In the next few days, you're taken to a detention center. You have a hearing before a judge. The judge orders you to be deported. Your wife and baby visit you before you leave.

"I'll try to get back as soon as I can," you tell your wife. You kiss your baby good-bye.

You're flown back to Mexico. You return to your mother's house to start all over again. You want to save money to hire a coyote to get you across the border again. But if you are caught entering illegally, you face 20 years in prison. The risks of returning are great.

THE END

To follow another path, turn to page 11.
To read the conclusion, turn to page 101.

"Jorge, I think I would rather stay here with my cousin. The work at the plant is steady."

You report for work each day. You get good reports from your supervisors. In fact, your reviews are so good that you are recommended for a management position. You don't have to clean machines anymore. With the extra money, you rent your own apartment. You are also able to bring your mother and siblings to the United States. You're very happy to be together again.

98

THE END

To follow another path, turn to page 11.
To read the conclusion, turn to page 101.

For many miles, a fence separates the countries of Mexico and the United States.

You don't want to take the chance of getting caught. You think it's best to return home with what you have.

Your family is happy to see you. But the money you made doesn't last more than a few months. You find yourself back where you started. Your brothers and sisters must work instead of going to school. You make plans to go back to the States.

THE END

To follow another path, turn to page 11.
To read the conclusion, turn to page 101.

This sign is painted with the question, "How many more?" People worry about the dangers immigrants face trying to enter the United States.

CHAPTER 5

MEXICAN AMERICANS

For more than 100 years, Mexicans have turned to the United States for the opportunity of a better life. Hundreds of thousands of Mexicans cross the border each year. But crossing is not easy. The Rio Grande River, the hot desert, and uncaring smugglers are dangers to immigrants' safety. Each year, hundreds of immigrants die while attempting to enter the United States. In 2006, more than 500 immigrants lost their lives. That number was the highest ever.

Immigration reform is a hot topic among U.S. citizens and politicians. Some argue the border should be open to anyone who wants to work or live in the United States. Others believe the border needs to be protected. They say an unprotected border invites terrorists to sneak into the United States through Mexico.

No matter their views on immigration, Americans have been influenced by immigrants. Mexicans have brought with them their culture and heritage. Their way of life has become a part of the larger U.S. culture.

Dancers celebrate their Mexican heritage at Cinco de Mayo festivals in the United States.

People with Mexican immigrant backgrounds have made great contributions to the United States. Former Attorney General Alberto Gonzalez is the son of migrant workers. Gonzalez was the nation's top lawyer from 2005 to 2007. Loretta and Linda Sanchez are the first sisters ever to serve in the U.S. House of Representatives. They are the daughters of Mexican immigrant parents. Writer Sandra Cisneros uses the experiences of her Mexican immigrant father in her books.

Mexican immigrants and their sons and daughters live and work all around the United States. They have made many contributions to the culture, to government, and to citizens' everyday lives.

Coming to the United States is a difficult choice for many Mexicans.

In the States, Mexicans find opportunities they might not otherwise have in their home country. As long as there is a chance for "life, liberty, and the pursuit of happiness," Mexican immigration is sure to continue.

Time Line

1848 — After the Mexican War, Mexico gives much of the present-day southwestern territory to the United States. Mexicans living in the area become U.S. citizens.

1910 — Thousands of Mexicans come to the States seeking safety during the Mexican Revolution.

1917 — Congress passes the Immigrant Act, which requires that immigrants be able to read and write.

1924 — Congress approves the Immigration Act. This law limits the number of immigrants allowed to enter the country. Congress also establishes the U.S. Border Patrol.

1930s — During the Great Depression, the U.S. government forces thousands of Mexicans, even those who are U.S. citizens, back to Mexico during a repatriation program.

1942 — The Bracero program begins, allowing Mexican workers to come into the States for temporary jobs, mostly in agriculture.

1954 — The U.S. Immigration Service launches "Operation Wetback," in which 3.8 million Mexicans are sent back to Mexico.

1962 — Cesar Chavez organizes the National Farm Workers Association, later called the United Farm Workers (UFW).

1975 — California passes the Agricultural Labor Relations Act (ALRA), giving farmworkers more rights.

1986 — Congress passes the Immigration Reform and Control Act. Some undocumented workers are allowed to become legal.

1994 — Voters in California approve Proposition 187, denying education, health care, and benefits to illegal immigrants. Despite voter approval, the courts do not allow it to ever take effect.

1996 — Congress passes the Illegal Immigration Reform and Immigrant Responsibility Act, which toughens penalties for illegal immigrants.

1999 — "Operation Vanguard" is launched by the Immigration and Naturalization Service. The goal is to prevent companies from knowingly hiring illegal workers.

2007 — The Senate fails to pass the DREAM (Development, Relief, and Education for Alien Minors) Act. The law would have allowed illegal immigrants younger than age 30 to become legal if they attend college or join the military.

OTHER PATHS
TO EXPLORE

In this book, you've seen how the events experienced by Mexican immigrants look different from three points of view.

Perspectives on history are as varied as the people who lived it. You can explore other paths on your own to learn more about what happened. Seeing history from many points of view is an important part of understanding it.

Here are some ideas for other Mexican immigration points of view to explore:

♦ Mexican immigrants often leave their families behind when they come to America. What is it like to stay in Mexico, waiting for money?

♦ Fruit and vegetable growers paid low wages to Mexican workers. If you were a grower in the 1970s, how would you have treated the migrant workers?

♦ Any child born in the United States is a U.S. citizen. What would it be like to have parents who are illegal immigrants?

READ MORE

Haugen, Brenda. *Cesar Chavez: Crusader for Social Change.* Minneapolis: Compass Point Books, 2008.

Ingram, Scott. *Mexican Americans.* Milwaukee: World Almanac Library, 2007.

Schroeder, Michael J. *Mexican Americans.* New York: Chelsea House, 2007.

Worth, Richard. *Mexican Immigrants.* New York: Facts on File, 2005.

INTERNET SITES

FactHound offers a safe, fun way to find Internet sites related to this book. All of the sites on FactHound have been researched by our staff.

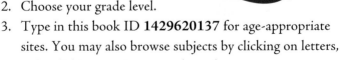

Here's how:
1. Visit *www.facthound.com*
2. Choose your grade level.
3. Type in this book ID **1429620137** for age-appropriate sites. You may also browse subjects by clicking on letters, or by clicking on pictures and words.
4. Click on the **Fetch It** button.

FactHound will fetch the best sites for you!

GLOSSARY

boycott (BOY-kot) — to refuse to buy or use a product or service to protest something believed to be wrong or unfair

consulate (KON-suh-luht) — the building where the consul is stationed in a foreign country; the consul is the person who processes visa requests.

deport (di-PORT) — to send people back to their own country

detention center (di-TEN-shuhn SEN-tur) — a place where people suspected of a crime are held

recruiter (ri-KROOT-uhr) — a person who hires workers for a company

smuggle (SMUHG-uhl) — to bring something or someone into or out of a country illegally

110

strike (STRIKE) — to refuse to work because of a disagreement with an employer over wages or working conditions

union (YOON-yuhn) — an organized group of workers that tries to gain better pay and working conditions

visa (VEE-zuh) — a document giving a person permission to enter a foreign country

BIBLIOGRAPHY

Ashabranner, Brent. *Dark Harvest: Migrant Farmworkers in America.* New York: Dodd, Mead, 1985.

Heaps, Willard A. *Wandering Workers: The Story of American Migrant Farm Workers and Their Problems.* New York: Crown, 1968.

Hondagneu-Sotelo, Pierrette. *Doméstica: Immigrant Workers Cleaning and Caring in the Shadows of Affluence.* Berkeley, Calif.: University of California Press, 2001.

Immigrant Law Center of Minnesota http://www.immigrantlawcentermn.org/ilcm.htm

Nazario, Sonia. *Enrique's Journey.* New York: Random House, 2006.

Pew Hispanic Center http://pewhispanic.org

Quinones, Sam. *Antonio's Gun and Delfino's Dream: True Tales of Mexican Migration.* Albuquerque, N.M.: University of New Mexico Press, 2007.

INDEX